# after-dinner drinks

RYLAND
PETERS
& SMALL
LONDON NEW YORK

# after-dinner drinks

*discovering, exploring, enjoying*

**Andrew Jefford**

Photography by William Lingwood

**Senior Designer** Steve Painter
**Editor** Miriam Hyslop
**Production** Louise Bartrum
**Art Director** Gabriella Le Grazie
**Publishing Director** Alison Starling

**Stylist** Helen Trent
**Photographer's Assistant** Emma Bentham-Wood

First published in the United States in 2003
by Ryland Peters & Small, Inc.
519 Broadway
5th Floor
New York NY10012
www.rylandpeters.com

10 9 8 7 6 5 4 3 2 1

Library of Congress Cataloging-in-Publication Data

Jefford, Andrew.
  After-dinner drinks : discovering, exploring, enjoying / Andrew
Jefford.
     p. cm.
  ISBN 1-84172-508-0
  1.  Alcoholic beverages.  I. Title.
  TX951.J43 2003
  641.8'74--dc21
                               2003008799

Printed in China.

# contents

# enjoyment ... and digestion

This is a book about forms of pure pleasure. No one need ever take an after-dinner drink: appetite has, by then, long been satisfied. What you sip, once dinner is over, feeds the senses and the soul rather than the body.

Or almost. If the drinks which follow do have a nutritive purpose, it is that of helping the body absorb and metabolize what has gone before. What is the best way to do this? By the quiet mechanisms of delight; by the subtle responses of contentment. There are no more dishes to match, no more combinations to try. No after-dinner drink ever need be finished at a sitting, so over-indulgence (though understandable) is never necessary or justified. Only pleasure counts now.

That may be one of the reasons why after-dinner drinks are so varied; that may be one of the reasons why so many of them are sweet. Their digestive origins account for the fact that the greatest liqueurs are based on ancient herbal elixirs; it is the reason, too, why many contain a charge of bitter herbs and plants ... which their sugar in turn helps balance and render palatable. Liqueurs of more recent invention offer a synopsis of fruit flavors; the latest successes draw on the richness of cream, too.

After-dinner wines, like port and madeira, use spirit to fix natural grape sugars and prevent them fermenting: these are vineyard flavors given unprecedented power. Other drinks, like Scotch or cognac, are pure spirit alone, crafted by wood and by time. Distillation, here, has captured an essence, and in doing so, changed its raw material into a drink of exquisite durability.

# distillation

You need little background knowledge to enjoy after-dinner drinks. The main requirement is a nose and a mouth, and the enjoyment of their use. One piece of information, though, may be useful.

Many after-dinner drinks are spirits; all include some spirit among their ingredients. What, then, is spirit? The answer is that it is an alcoholic drink created by the process of distillation.

Distillation must, to its early medieval pioneers, have seemed an almost magical process, a kind of alchemy. They would have long been familiar with beer (a fermented drink made from grains) and wine (a fermented drink made from grapes or other fruits). By heating these drinks gently and gathering the steam they produced, it was possible to harvest their essence: a colorless liquid which burned the tongue and sent fire and elation coursing through the body. What had the pioneers discovered?

Fermented drinks like wine and beer contain a mixture of alcohol and water. Alcohol boils at 173°F (78.5°C); water boils at 212°F (100°C). If you heat a fermented drink, therefore, its alcohol will vaporize before its water does. Provide some sort of cool surface on which the alcohol vapor can precipitate, and you become a distiller.

That is the principle of all distillation. If you distill wine, you obtain brandy; if you distill beer, you obtain whiskey; if you distill hard cider, you obtain calvados or apple brandy. Rum is made from fermented sugar syrups, and neutral spirits such as vodka are based on a variety of fermented starchy substances including wheat, rye, corn, and potatoes.

# port

Port is a beautiful deviant. It begins life
no differently from any other wine—with
crushed fresh grapes and wine yeasts, which
float like dust motes in the air. Fermentation
begins. If nature was to take its course, the
now-seething juices would become dry table
wine. Instead, shortly before half-time, the
part-fermented wine is tipped into a vat of
chilled brandy. Fermentation stops,
immediately: the high alcoholic strength, a
sudden lunge from just 6% to 19%, kills the
yeasts. Yet the wine remains saturatedly
sweet—with vineyard sugars. The result,
provided the grapes dug their roots into the
rocky schist of Portugal's mountainous Douro
valley, is port.

*exuberant with sweet
blackberry and black currant*

*packed with fruit,*
*pepper, and fire*

## bottle-aged ports

There are two families of port:
the dark and the pale. Pale, orange-
russet ports are aged in wood, to
smooth and soften them, before
bottling (see opposite). Dark, red-
black ports, by contrast, are bottled
early, when they are still packed with
fruit, pepper, and fire.

The simplest ports on this dark side
of the family are called Ruby. Others,
with a little more belly, go to market
under a brand name like Cockburn's
Special Reserve or Graham's Six
Grapes. Vintage Character or Late-
Bottled Vintage are two further
descriptions: the former is blended
from the fruit of several vintages,
while the latter (in theory a slightly
better wine) is from a single year
only. The best of these "drink me"
dark ports are exuberant, with sweet
blackberry and black currant, coating

the tongue softly and leaving the
mouth humming with their cracked-
pepper fumes.

More forceful still are their grander,
unfiltered cousins: Traditional Late-
Bottled Vintage, Crusted port, and
Vintage port. Some come from a
single farm or *quinta*. The port-maker's
role consists in pounding (sometimes
by machine, but sometimes, too, by
soft human feet) as much matter
from the grape skins as possible in
the 22 hours or so before the part-
fermented wine plunges into the chill
brandy. The result is, almost literally,
explosive. Only time can ease the
tightly coiled flavors; one proof that it
has done so is the sediment in the
bottle. The other proof is in the glass.
The youthful black currant has
acquired a tea-caddy refinement; the
raw tannins have formed a gracefully
lithe skeleton; the mad power has
become sweet authority.

## wood-aged port

Dark ports are tamed in glass; pale ports slumber their way towards maturity in wooden casks called *pipas* or "pipes," which contain 141 gallons (534 liters) each. They are stored in large, roomy lodges on the banks of the River Douro at Vila Nova de Gaia, opposite Porto itself (the town that gives the wine its name). It's shady inside these lodges; occasionally a sunbeam cascades through a cobwebby window, or slides through the gap left by a missing roof tile, but in the main, a comfortable gloom prevails. The still air fills with the scent of raisins, of figs, of roses, of dust itself.

Ports of this type are bottled when they are ready to drink, and require no further storage. Tawny port, Colheita port (vintage-dated tawny) and port with an indication of age (10 Years Old, 20 Years Old, 30 Years Old, and Over 40 Years Old) all fall into this category. Young and inexpensive examples are a light garnet in color and still hint at fresh fruits, though strawberry is a more likely note than black currant or bramble. Old versions, by contrast, are tangier, given bite and edge by half a human lifetime's contact with air and with wooden staves. The scents now hint at nuts, at vanilla, at old libraries and fine furniture; the flavors now cover the figgy sweetness which time cannot erode with a shawl of dried peach and apricot. All is glycerol and harmony after so long a wait.

## storing and serving port

The only ports you are ever likely to have to store yourself are the unfiltered grandees on the dark side of the family: Traditional Late-Bottled Vintage port, Crusted port and Vintage port, including those from a single *quinta* or farm. All other ports are sold when ready to drink, and require no further storage. Those ports which reward long keeping (Vintage port is generally ready to drink from its fifteenth birthday onwards, while the others need ten years or so) should be placed on their sides in a dark place where there are few temperature fluctuations. Don't forget to stand them up again before you want to drink them. The loose sediment, often copious, will then slide down to the bottom of the bottle, which will make decanting easier.

**What is decanting?** Simply this: pouring the wine carefully off its sediment in order to leave it clear and bright. You don't even need a special serving vessel, though a gleamingly filled decanter makes a handsome sight; it is quite enough to pour the clear wine into a pitcher, rinse out the bottle, then pour the wine back into its familiar home. Try to pour the wine close to a light source like a candle or electric light so that you can see the exact moment at which the sediment begins to move with the wine.

The dark side of the family is best served at cool room temperature; 66°F (19°C) is ideal. The paler ports, by contrast, appreciate a chill before serving, especially the younger ones. If you want to drink port in the summer, chilled tawny (with, ideally, a dish of roasted almonds) is delicious.

# dessert sherry

Sherry, like port, is a combination of wine and spirit; it differs from port in that the spirit is added at the end of fermentation, not halfway through. Meaning? Yes, that's right: all classic sherry styles begin life dry. If you're going to have a glass of sherry after dinner, though, the chances are that you'll want a sweet sherry. To make the best of these, very old dry sherries are blended with small amounts of unctuously sweet sherry, often made from grapes dried in the sun before vinification. The best are then aged once again for many further years. The result is as intricate and elaborate as any Moorish palace.

## discovering dessert sherry

Dry sherry is made in one of two ways. Fino or Manzanilla sherry is aged biologically (by the action of a blanket of yeast which forms naturally on the wine, called *flor*); Oloroso sherry is aged chemically (by oxidation). Amontillado and Palo Cortado sherries have been aged by a combination of both methods. The result is an orchestra of different scents and flavors, of forms of tanginess, of allusions to nuts and leaves, to sea breezes and dried fruits. But age, for dry sherry, brings a burden of bitterness. Which is where Pedro Ximenez comes in.

Pedro Ximenez is sherry's sweet grape; all the dry wines are made from Palomino. On its own, "PX" barely resembles wine at all; it's more like a syrup of raisins (the locals love to pour it on ice cream). Black in color, it looks like engine oil. Mix it with those old dry sherries, though, and it suddenly seems to open up a new landscape of possibilities.

Taste a great sweet sherry like Matusalem from Gonzalez Byass, Sibarita from Pedro Domecq, or Solera 1842 from Valdespino, and the sometimes austere and piercing flavors of old dry sherries become carnivals for the nose and mouth in which the old and the burnt spring back into life, refreshed by a rain of dark sweetness. New-style sweet sherries, paler in color, are sweetened with Moscatel rather than PX, giving grapier, more freshly fruited flavors: these are the so-called "pale creams."

# madeira

Madeira, like port and sherry, is a fortified wine. It is grown and made on the lush, fecund Atlantic island of Madeira. Sweet madeira (like port) is fortified part-way through fermentation; dry madeira (like sherry), after fermentation. Then something uniquely odd happens to madeira. It is heated. Less expensive madeira is gently cooked in a giant tank for three months; this process is known as *estufagem*. Great madeira is, by contrast, aged in casks in warm attics for at least three years, and often many more; this process is called *canteiro*. The more expensive the madeira, the more likely it is to be made, in whole or in part, by the *canteiro* method.

*no other wine allows you to build up a reference library of scents and flavors as madeira does*

## discovering madeira

I mentioned on the opposite page that madeira is, uniquely, made by heat. It has another secret, too. The passing of time is, for this wine, more important than for any other.

Young madeira is dull and mawkish. With every year that passes, though, it acquires interest, eventually grandeur. Old vintage madeira ("Vintage" wines can't even be bottled before their twentieth birthday) is among the most intense and architecturally extravagant wines in existence. The long, hot aging process it has passed through in the sun-warmed attics of Funchal gives it a shot at immortality. Once opened, the wine will last for months without spoiling. A sip lingers for minutes on the tongue. If I have one piece of advice for you about madeira, it is to try the oldest (thus, alas, the most expensive) you can afford.

Grape varieties generally indicate sweetness on Madeira. If no grape variety is mentioned on the bottle, then the wine will be made from the island's all-purpose grape, Tinta Negra Mole. Look out for soft, tangy flavors with, in this case, varying levels of sweetness which the label should indicate. If the madeira in your glass is made from any other grape, then the relevant variety will be named on the label. Sercial is driest, sometimes austerely so, with tongue-slicing acidity. Verdelho is less dry, full of tantalizing orchard delicacy: it makes an invigorating mid-afternoon revivor. Bual and Malmsey are both sweet. Bual is nutty, burnished, and elegant, while Malmsey—a broader, fatter wine— strokes in layers of chocolate and raisin. You may very rarely see the names Terrantez or Bastardo on a bottle of madeira: these two ancient varieties are, like Bual and Malmsey, made in a sweet style.

## storing and serving madeira

All madeira is sold when it is ready to drink. You never need store it. As I mentioned on the previous page, though, madeira can come closer to achieving immortality than any other wine, so you may want to hide away a special Vintage bottle for a decade or two. Unusually, madeira can be stored upright (as it is on the island). It will also tolerate variations in temperature better than any other wine, though a cool cellar is ideal.

Madeira is not in a hurry; madeira is never in a hurry. It loves air and time. Pour a small amount into a large glass, and swirl it well. If it's good, you will find one set of aromas after five minutes, another set after twenty, and yet more two hours later. Great madeira is a kind of slow, vinous firework. As I mentioned earlier, you can drink a quarter of a bottle, then put the cork back in and leave it for three weeks without it deteriorating in quality. No other wine allows you to build up a reference library of scents and flavors as

madeira does. The intensity of the very greatest madeiras, finally, is such that even relatively small quantities will sing in the mouth for long minutes. These are some of the ways in which its expense can come to seem good value.

Madeira's sediment is never more than light, but its hunger for air often makes decanting worthwhile. Good madeira never needs chilling; a room temperature of 68°F (20°C) or so is ideal to allow it to unfold calmly, even the drier Sercial and Verdelho styles.

*great madeira is a kind of slow, vinous firework*

# scotch whisky

Whisky (or whiskey if it's an American or Irish distillation), as we discovered on page seven, is distilled beer. If the process takes place in Scotland, and if the resulting spirit is aged for at least three years in wooden casks before being sold, then it can call itself Scotch whisky—or Scotch, for short. There are many whiskies in the world, but none tastes like Scotch. The way in which the grains are prepared; the use of old (not new) wood for aging the liquor; the pristine quality of Scottish water, and the country's cool, moist air all play a role. So, too, do distillery and blending skills, as the products of 103 whisky distilleries are brought together like paints on a canvas within bottles of Scotland's nourishing, golden spirit.

## blended scotch

The world of Scotch is divided into two families: malts and blends. Over 95% of all the Scotch sold around the world is blended; it includes great drams like the succulent Johnnie Walker Red Label, the heathery, elegant Famous Grouse, or the smoky, ember-like Black Bottle. What defines them?

Scotch can be distilled in two different ways. Malt whisky, which is made from malted barley only, is double distilled in pot stills, just like cognac. Grain whisky, which is made from wheat and corn, plus a small amount of malted barley, is distilled in towering continuous stills on an industrial scale. (There are 96 working malt whisky distilleries in Scotland at present, but only seven grain distilleries.) If you mix malt whisky together with grain whisky, the result is a "blend." It may be less characterful and less pungent than a pure (or "single") malt, but it is also less expensive. Many drinkers, too, find blends easier to drink. They tend to be creamier, softer, lighter, smoother, and more caressing. For this reason, they mix more readily with other drinks, too.

Most blends are drunk before dinner, and most malts afterwards. There are, however, some blends which are intended for sipping and savoring at length, either because they contain a wide range of rare components, fastidiously blended; or because they are dark, old, and liquorous in style. Fine examples of these after-dinner blends include the sumptuous, multi-faceted Ballantine's 21-year-old; the plungingly deep, challenging, peat-fused Johnnie Walker Black Label, and the creamy, comely Johnnie Walker Gold Label, all satins and silks. Buchanan's 12- and 18-year-old blends are densely crafted, too.

## speyside malts

The great malt whiskies of Scotland are generally grouped together by regional origin. Why? The rule isn't a rigid one, but often whiskies which come from the same place share certain stylistic traits. This is particularly true of two distillery communities: that of Speyside in north-eastern Scotland, and that of the southern Hebridean island of Islay.

The river Spey is a fast, bright, tumbling run of water which dashes from the Highlands down into the gray Moray Firth. Once the river leaves Grantown, distilleries crowd its banks and those of its tributaries (like the Fiddich) and its sibling rivers (like the Deveron and the Lossie). This is Scotland at its briskest and driest. Come winter, frost will bite at the burns (streams), and snow lie mutely on the hills while the crows call each other for solace. In summer, by contrast, the rocks glow and the great oaks spread.

Speyside whiskies are, if you like, the classics of the Scotch malt world: firm, finely balanced, sometimes haughty, neither evidently peaty nor becomingly sweet but almost always something of both, this flesh draped lithely about a firm skeleton.

The world's biggest-selling malt, Glenfiddich, is among their number: pale, sappy, a soprano. At least when young; age brings a honeyed sweetness. Its sister distillery, Balvenie, is darker and more earthy. Cragganmore takes you for a walk in a dark forest; time in the glass uncovers shy spice. Glen Grant is fresh and zesty, while The Glenlivet is soft, brocaded, and floral. Longmorn is darker and oilier, a cloaked Speysider. Macallan, considered by many to be the finest of all, is a meal in a glass: richly fruited, resonant, a cascade of glowing coals.

*richly fruited, resonant, a cascade of glowing coals*

## islay malts

Islay (pronounced "Ila") is a damp, open island of bleak, cloud-gathering beauty which lies off the west coast of Scotland; the Ulster coast breaks from the sea just 25 miles away, making it a closer landfall than Glasgow. Islay boasts, at present, some seven distilleries; no other Scottish island has more than two. Chance? Hardly.

The Irish connection is telling, to begin with: whisky may well have passed to Scotland by this route. Unusually for a Hebridean island, large acreages of Islay are fertile enough to grow grain. Fresh water is abundant, lying deep in the bogs and falling from the sky. Islay has peat of magnificent quality, and lots of it. Finally, when it's time to age the malt, the salt-laden air and cool temperatures are perfect for ripening a wild whisky over ten or fifteen moist years into something more calmly succulent, more civilly savage.

What is malt? It is sprouted barley. The raw grain does not yield fermentable sugars; only malted grain does. You need warmth and moisture to start the malting process, and heat to stop it. Islay's peaty whiskies gain their scent and flavor not from the bog-brown stain in their water, but from the peat smoke which billows through the malt as it is kilned and dried.

Ardbeg, Lagavulin, and Laphroaig are the island's three peatiest whiskies at present, though more (like Port Charlotte and Octomore) will follow. Ardbeg is densest and most tight-knit; Lagavulin richest and lushest; Laphroaig smokiest and saltiest, a true sea-creature. Sculpted, gracious Bowmore and lighter, hospital-clean Caol Ila are less extravagantly peaty; the almondy, creamy Bruichladdich and sinewy, cockleshell Bunnahabhain show Islay in a paler, breezier mood.

## other malts

Away from Speyside and Islay, malt whisky distilleries are sparse and widely scattered in Scotland. Bladnoch in Galloway lies some 300 miles from Highland Park on Orkney; a distillery is planned for Shetland, 100 miles north again. It is hard to speak of regional character when a distillery is a singleton; a character of its own, of course, is something every distillery has.

Dalwhinnie is Scotland's highest distillery; there will be some days every year during which drifted snow make it impossible to reach. Up here among the deer, the bare peaks, and the icy lochs, you'll find a whisky of light, dancing, heathery, aerial character. Glenmorangie, at Tain in the Northern Highlands, is every bit as graceful yet, in place of Dalwhinnie's honeyed charms, you'll find a malt packed with cut-grass freshness and bluebell scent. Oban is a sea-captain's town, the gateway to the isles: its buoyant and sprightly whisky shares some of that briskness and brio. Springbank is one of just two survivors of the great Campbeltown distilling tradition, now largely lost; this briny malt, scything in its dry intensity, shows us just how much we might be missing. The peaty Longrow comes from the same stills.

Finally, come two great malts from islands other than Islay. Talisker is made at the head of one of Skye's remoter sea lochs, facing the Outer Hebrides: it is a forceful, jangling, wild, and pummelling dram. Highland Park on Orkney, by contrast, is full of sober, quiet yet provoking grandeur, its restrained peat notes lending it reverberatively smoky depths.

# bourbon

Bourbon is a type of whiskey distilled in the USA, chiefly in Kentucky. It is made from a number of different grains: mostly corn (between 51% and 80%), complemented by malted barley, rye, and wheat. (Rye whiskey is made from at least 51% rye, and corn whiskey from more than 80% corn.) The initial beer is turned into spirit in continuous stills, complemented by refining "doublers;" above all, though, its flavor is conditioned by its aging process. Those sweet vanilla, mint, and violet scents reveal all. Bourbon must be aged for at least two years in new white oak casks, often heavily charred. Kentucky summers, moreover, are hot, further intensifying the all-important exchanges with the oak.

## discovering bourbon

Bourbon, as we have learned, can come from anywhere in the USA, but not all American whiskies choose to describe themselves thus. The biggest selling American whiskey of all, Jack Daniel's, proclaims itself a Tennessee whiskey, as does George Dickel (though Dickel favors the spelling "whisky"). Both use deep charcoal-filtering for extra creaminess and char-sweetness.

There are other terms used on labels, too. "Sour mash" means that a proportion of the spent grains, the final cereal residue, of the previous brew has been retained and added to the new brew (usually 25–30%). The word "straight" indicates that no coloring or flavoring has been added, and that (unless stated to the contrary) the liquor has been aged for four years or more.

And the flavor in all of this? Bourbon and Tennessee whiskey is, in general, less subtle and nuanced than Scotch—but when it comes to an after-dinner drink, you may think that's a good thing. These are sweetly exuberant, perfumed, uninhibited, and hedonistic whiskies. Jim Beam is one of the lightest; Heaven Hill is more complex and lush; Wild Turkey is honeyed and multi-layered, among the most flavorsome of all; Rebel Yell is powerful and penetrating; Woodford Reserve ripples with mint and orange. Of the two Tennessee whiskies, Jack Daniel's is frank, forthright, and full of sweet char, while Dickel is more delicate, dryer, and understated. Most ambitious of all is the nutty, spicy, smooth, and unctuous Maker's Mark (made with no rye at all). Straight rye whiskey is rarely seen outside the USA and little made inside it, but its fruity, punchy style makes a fine contrast to the lusher, sweeter, corn-rich bourbons.

# irish and other whiskies

Irish whiskey (this spelling is used) once eclipsed Scotch. Not so today: the country has only three distilleries. By far the biggest is Midleton in County Cork: it produces a wide range of spirits using both pot stills and continuous stills, and using both malt and unmalted grains. Bushmills on the Antrim coast, close to the geometric geology of the Giant's Causeway, has only pot stills, though its blends are mixed with grain whiskey from Midleton. Newest of the three is the Cooley distillery at Dundalk, on the border between Eire and Northern Ireland, where both pot stills and continuous stills are used.

The hallmark of much Irish whiskey is a soft, quenching grassiness, most clearly seen in the biggest-selling of Ireland's whiskies, Jameson, distilled and blended at Midleton. For after-dinner drinking, though, search out the creamy, spicy Power's and the dryer, deeper Redbreast (pure pot still, though not a pure malt—unmalted grains are also used). Look out, too, for Jameson's more ambitious siblings, Crested 10 and 1780. The Bushmills style is brisker and more thrusting, seen best in the raisiny, spicy Black Bush blend and the dry, penetrating 16-year-old Single Irish Malt. The Tyrconnell, named

after a celebrated 100–1 winner of the Irish Classic, leads the Cooley brands: it's a lighter, grassier, and younger malt than that of Bushmills. Connemara is a peated malt from Cooley, while sweet, soft Kilbeggan is its leading blend.

Many other countries, of course, produce whiskey. Canada's are gentle and unintimidating multi-grain spirits, distilled by a variety of techniques, and then blended. Japan's fine pot-still whiskies are generally blended with Scottish malts before sale, though some "singles" (like Yoichi and Yamazaki) exist.

# cognac

Just as whiskey is made by distilling beer, so brandy is made by distilling wine. Wherever wine is made, you will also find brandy. Nowhere, though, will you find a brandy which can rival cognac for perfumed finesse. One sip, once swallowed, seems to vaporize into nature's essences—the scents of pounded stones, of gathered flowers, of the beehive, of fallen fruits on a sunny path. How does cognac do this? Not by method; there are other brandies made with the same care. Cognac is a place: a sunny, quiet, white-soiled pasture-land in western France. Only from here can "burnt wine" grow, with time, as subtle.

## stone and sun

It was salt, first of all; later, grain and butter. Wine, in the Middle Ages, came a poor fourth among the reasons for ships to anchor at La Rochelle or Royan. Thin and tart, it was. Better to press on up the Gironde to Bordeaux; better to bargain for Cahors.

By Shakespeare's times, distillation was beginning to change matters. The Dutch were keen on what they called *brandewijn*, burnt wine: they brought copper south from Sweden to make stills, and returned to Amsterdam with the spirit which ran from them. It took less space in the hold, and survived July heat and February storms. As the years passed, too, thousands of North Europeans reached, by tavern candlelight, a common conclusion: brandy from hereabouts was uncommonly good. Ask for it by name. We still do: cognac.

Why? Chalk, to begin with: alkaline mineral food for vines which (as in Champagne, as in Chablis) make wines of purity and edge. No shortage of wood, either, in this easily managed landscape, to fire stills, to house new liquor. Add to that the climate: sweet, luminous, and still.

Great spirit is the product of air as well as earth, and cognac loves its calm cosseting in the vapory riverside warehouses of the Charente.

There are six sub-zones within Cognac; the names of the three best, Grande Champagne, Petite Champagne, and Borderies, may be found on labels. (Fine Champagne is a blend of Grande and Petite.) Why Champagne? Back in Shakespeare's day, it was a general term to describe open country. "Daylight and champaign discovers not more!" cries Malvolio in *Twelfth Night*. The meaning, like cognac itself, has dawdled down time.

## discovering cognac

As we learned on page 31, cognac can come from one of six areas. It is made every year; no two vintages are alike. It needs time: at least three years for three star or VS. VSOP from most houses has eight or ten years; XO, 20 or more; and the most expensive cognacs of all will have been distilled some 40 or 50 years before the bottles finally take flight for the duty-free shops of Tokyo or Singapore.

This original complexity—of exact origin, of vintage, and of years passed inside casks (new or old) made from tight-grained Limousin or Tronçais oak—is not reflected, but refracted and reassembled, in the bottles we buy. Enthusiasts may seek out the single-vineyard cognacs of farmer-distillers; vintage cognac may be with us in future years; but for the time being, most of the great cognacs are compounded, by nose alone, in sample-lined blending rooms. There are differences of style. Martell is floral yet forceful; Courvoisier, rich; Rémy-Martin, lively and fruited; Hennessy, full and earthy. My own favorite, Hine, is layered and intricate, as packed with perfumed allusions as a cathedral is with whispers. Delamain is light, a silk scarf: pure nuance.

The cognac world, though, is changing. As it must: sales have declined sharply. Traditional variations on the theme include Early Landed Cognacs—those aged not in the sunny air of the Charente, but in the dampness of Bristol or London (the style is more delicate and graceful). A newer approach comes from Hennessy: Pure White. Less oak; more mixability.

*layered and intricate,*
*as packed with perfumed allusions*
*as a cathedral is with whispers*

# armagnac

Armagnac is, with cognac, one of France's two great brandies. Whereas cognac is elegant and refined, a spirit in which aromas and flavors glint off each other like light off a chandelier, armagnac is an exuberant, sometimes gruff spirit summary of the French countryside. Smoke and earth provide its hallmark notes, and licking fire is never far behind; you may also find prune, wild mushroom, and leather in its exuberant, bear-hug embrace. There is no better brandy anywhere in the world for keeping the cold at bay, and keeping the darkness of winter lit.

## stone and sun

Armagnac's home is in Gascony—where rugby is preferred to soccer, where wild boar ruck after roots in the oakwoods, and where the possession of a pigeon-shooting tree-house called a *palombière* is of far more consequence than the keys to a new BMW.

In contrast to the pure chalky soils of Cognac, most armagnac is grown on darker, richer earth. The region has three zones. The most deeply flavored, fiery, and thrusting armagnacs come from the sand and clay-soiled Bas-Armagnac. Ténarèze includes some limestone, and its spirit tends to be a little dryer, more elegant and more flowery than in Bas-Armagnac. Haut-Armagac, finally, produces lighter spirit than either, and is sparsely planted. Most armagnac is a blend from the first two zones.

It is not just stone and sun, though, which accounts for the bonfire-like impact a glass of armagnac can have on your digestive system. Whereas cognac is double-distilled in pot stills to a strength of 70% or so, most armagnac is distilled in small continuous stills to a strength of just 52% to 65%. The higher the strength to which you distill a liquor, the "purer"—and less flavorful—it will be. (Vodka, distilled to 96%, proves the point.) Armagnac's relatively low distillation strength ensures that all the countryside overtones it can muster will survive the metamorphosis of distillation. It does, though, mean that most armagnac needs long aging before it is ready to drink. A young white alternative called Blanche, distilled to a higher strength and aged only in stainless steel and glass, is imminent.

What about grapes, finally? Armagnac also uses Ugni Blanc, the grape which creates cognac, but in contrast to cognac, a hybrid grape called Baco, and the ancient Folle Blanche variety, both contribute to its rousing, male-voice chorus.

## discovering armagnac

The fact that Armagnac is not dominated by large producers in the way that Cognac is makes it more complicated to discover—but more rewarding, too.

The region's largest producer, Janneau, is in some ways one of the least typical, since it uses only pot stills and not the traditional continuous armagnac still. It then blends its own pot-still liquor with continuously distilled purchases. The result is a series of forthright and forceful spirits in which the warm regional style emerges with clean, frank poise.

Comte de Lauvia and Marquis de Montesquiou are two other larger, reliable names (the blends are the same): the XO, in particular, is sweetly exotic and unusually seductive for armagnac.

The greatest armagnacs of all, though, are some of the often ancient "Hors d'Age" and vintage liquors produced by the region's very best grower-distillers. Gérard Laberdolive of Domaine d'Escoubes, the Lafitte family of Domaine Boignères, the Comte de Boisséson of Château de Lacquy: in the farmhouses of family companies like these lie well-stocked spirit libraries, the legacy of their forbears. In place of book after book and page after page, each grower guards a huge repository of scents and flavors. From time to time, when customers beg or when domestic finances oblige, a few bottles are filled and dispatched to a distant but appreciative world.

Do not expect great consistency from vintage armagnac: that is not the point. Each year is different from every other, and so is each barrel. Some are light; others are dark and thunderous. Older does not necessarily mean better. What you will find, though, are allusions to a fecund, autumnal world: the scent of nuts, of fallen leaves, of toffee, of cooked orange, of moist prune. And, of course, the glowing fire beyond.

# other
# brandies

Wherever wine is made, brandy will be distilled. France's two great brandies may be the world's most celebrated, but Spain, South Africa, Mexico, Chile, Peru, and the USA are important brandy-producing nations, too. Styles vary greatly, depending on the grape varieties used to make the base wine, on the distillation process, and on the type of wood-maturation the liquor receives. True brandy is made by distilling wine, but the term is also poached by other drinks such as eaux de vie ("plum brandy" and "apple brandy" are two examples) or liqueurs (like "cherry brandy" or "apricot brandy"). These names, though traditional, are misnomers.

## discovering brandy

France's greatest rival in brandy production is its Iberian neighbor, Spain. Indeed, it was the Spaniards who taught the French how to distill brandy, having themselves learned the art from their Moorish conquerors towards the end of the first millennium. Spain, today, has two official brandy denominations: Brandy del Penedès and, most importantly, Brandy de Jerez. The style of the older, grander Brandy de Jerez marques like Cardenal Mendoza, Lepanto, or Gran Duque d'Alba, is richly vanillic, as voluptuous and comforting as a deep leather armchair, and pungent with raisiny, sherryish overtones. Younger brandies, like Domecq's celebrated Fundador, are lighter and more fiery.

Elsewhere in Europe, Greece's Metaxa range tends to be sweet and toothsome, made by blending brandy with Muscat wine. German Asbach brandy is light, spicy, and oaky; Italy's Vecchia Romagna is smoother and softer, and Stock, a little dryer; fine brandies, too, come from Armenia's Ararat distillery. The world's biggest selling brandy is Mexico's Presidente, smooth and unexceptional; more interesting by far are the Pisco brandies of Chile and Peru. Many of these are made from aromatic grape varieties like Moscatel, giving them an appealingly perfumed quality which has little to do, for once, with oak aging.

South Africa's long history of brandy distillation means that the country's top pot-still spirits, produced by the giant KWV cooperative as well as smaller producers like Backsberg, are concentrated and long-flavored. America's traditionally bland brandies, the work of large companies like Gallo and Masson, are now being challenged by much better brandies from smaller, more ambitious producers like Alambic or Jepson.

# calvados

Any fermented drink can be distilled to make a spirit essence, and hard cider is no exception. The result is generally called apple brandy or applejack. If the hard cider (and perry, fermented from pears) is grown in the best apple orchards of Normandy in France, then the spirit can call itself calvados. The ghosts of thousands of cider apples hover over younger versions, filling them with sweetly breezy orchard scent; older versions, by contrast, are more marked by their slow years of cask confinement. The difference between a fine old calvados and an equally venerable armagnac is less marked than you might think.

## discovering calvados

There is one important principle of distillation that I haven't explained yet. It is this: acidity and sweetness do not survive distillation. Hard cider is, of course, often sharp, and often sweet too (though the cider used for distillation is dry). None of that acidity ever emerges at the other end of the still. When you pour yourself a glass of calvados, therefore, it is truly an essence of apple, rather than an essence of cider, which will greet you.

Some 40 varieties of cider apples and perry pears are allowed to be used to make calvados. In the best calvados-growing area of Normandy, the Pays d'Auge, distillation of the cider is by pot-still only, as for cognac and Scotch malt whisky; in other regions, continuous stills can also be used. The specialty of the Domfrontais appellation is that the spirit here is distilled from at least 30% perry. The new, clear spirit is then aged for at least a year, and usually for three or four. VSOP and Extra signifies an aging period of between five and ten years, while Hors d'Age and Age Inconnu are older still. Vintage calvados, hugely variable in style, is also sold.

Like armagnac, calvados is dominated by medium-sized and small-scale producers, each of whom guard their precious stocks for many years. Boulard is one of the best of the larger names: its apples and pears come from the Pays d'Auge alone, grown in Boulard's own orchards and those of its 500 grower-suppliers. Its most memorable spirit is the complex and fragrant XO. Fine spirit also comes from Camut (limpid and pure), Coeur de Lion (more marked by oak) and Dupont (driving dry intensity). From the Domfrontais, look out for Lemorton, whose spirit is distilled from twice as much perry as cider.

# aged rum

Rum is made from sugar. It can be based on fresh sugar cane juice (as French *rhum agricole* is); much, though, is derived from sugar cane syrup (boiled cane juice) or molasses (the dark residues of sugar production). This sweet liquid is fermented, and the resulting "beer" distilled in either pot stills or continuous stills. Depending on the chosen raw ingredients and distillation method, the rum produced will be light, heavy, or something between the two. It will also, of course, be colorless: color comes with cask age (or with the addition of caramel). The best after-dinner rums tend to be aged, and are heavier and darker than those used for mixing.

## discovering aged rum

Few spirits are as diverse as rum. Much of that diversity, though, is hidden. Rum is produced throughout the tropics, often on small islands and by small nations, yet access to the drinking markets is controlled by large brands, large companies, and large nations. The result is that most rum reaches us in pre-blended form, with the component parts of the blend sometimes coming from several different countries many thousands of miles apart. The "single malts" of the rum world are a tantalizing prospect for the future.

We may be waiting to discover the fecund intricacy of the Caribbean and its tropical neighbors, but there are still some excellent after-dinner rums to enjoy in the meantime. From Jamaica, for example, comes the Appleton Estate 12-year-old, a well-aged blend of spicy, smoky drive. Martinique's J. Bally Estate produces some fine vintage rums, sweet and sumptuous, as does the Clément distillery, whose "Très Vieux" vintage rums have hints of peel and zest, nuts and flowers behind the brown sugar depths. Haiti's leading producer sells its pot-still rum under the Barbancourt name: look out for the aristocratically

harmonious and refined Réserve du Domaine. Guyana's El Dorado Special Reserve is multi-layered and nuanced, gentler in style than many aged rums; while from Barbados comes the languid, palpably oaky Mount Gay Extra Old. Havana Club is Cuba's leading brand, and the Extra Aged 15-year-old is a fine sipping rum.

Cachaça is the name of Brazil's native rum, distilled like *rhum agricole* from fermented sugar cane juice. Most are designed to be mixed into a caipirinha cocktail, but among those which can be sipped on their own is the pot-still 10-year-old from Germana.

# aged tequila

You won't find a more unusual raw material for an alcoholic drink than the agave hearts from which tequila is made. The blue agave is a member of the lily family. It lolls idly in Mexico's dry, dusty, semi-desert earth, hidden by its soaring, spine-spiked leaves, for up to a decade. The harvested hearts are woody and inedible; only after a day and a half's slow cooking can they be made to yield a muddy soup capable of being fermented. Distil the brew, though, and suddenly a liquor emerges which seems to summarize the heart of the Americas, with its scents of baked chiles and sweet peppers, of stable, hide, and beaten earth.

## discovering aged tequila

As with rum, much tequila is bottled soon after distillation, white and pungent from the still; this boisterous, sappy infant is used to make cocktails and long drinks. The tequila most suitable for after-dinner sipping, by contrast, is older and darker—though tequila absorbs flavors from wooden casks as easily as sponges absorb water. While most liquors can take ten or twelve years in cask without losing any of their character, just two months makes a difference for tequila (this is the aging period specified for the *reposado* category). The classic sipping category of *añejo* tequila must spend a year in cask. Most producers exceed this, but call a halt to the process at five years or so. After that, the wood dominates, suffocating the hot desert scents and flavors of the agave.

Look for tequilas which describe themselves as "100% agave" or "100% agave azul," since they are made from pure agave; simple tequila without this qualification is made from just 51% agave, with the rest of the sugar for the ferment coming from cane. The result is a blander spirit. Among the best aged tequilas are the oily, buttery Chinaco Añejo; the mellow Don Julio Reserva; the complex and refined El Tesoro Añejo (also sold as Tapatio), one of the few in which those palpable pepper and vegetable notes of young tequila endure and deepen; the surprisingly delicate (and beautifully labeled) José Cuervo Reserva de la Familia; and the vanillic Porfidio Single Barrel Añejo.

*the taste of great vineyards,*
                                          *the print of place …*

# marc

The new season's wine is made; it rests in winter stillness. Outside, an early dusk sinks pinkly about the leafless vines. What remains? It's called pomace: a pile of grape skins and grape seeds. Good wine is made by gentle pressing. Gentle pressing means that those skins and seeds are still pregnant with aroma, with flavor, and (once fermented) with alcohol. Take them to the still, lift the life-print from these tired remnants with steam, and the wine grower can revive his exhausted arms, aching after a day's hard pruning, with pungent, warming spirit. This distillate of leftovers is called marc.

## discovering marc

Marc gives the drinker a chance to drink a great wine twice. First, of course, as wine; afterwards as a fiery spirit drawing its character from the same sensual DNA. Every wine region in France produces its own marc, but those of Burgundy and Champagne are particularly memorable. The two main grape varieties of both regions are the same: Chardonnay and Pinot Noir. French marc, however, is rarely varietal. It is the taste of great vineyards, the print of place, which both distiller and drinker is searching for.

The rules state that the distillate for marc should not exceed 71% as it runs from the stills. Like Armagnac, though, marc is generally distilled to about 50% or 52%, and at this strength will contain many of the flavor-bringing impurities which distillation to a higher strength eliminates. Young marc, thus, can be a challenging drink, almost uncomfortably characterful: pungent and bruising. The greatest, by contrast, will pass many years in cask to tame their exuberance and temper their excesses. A fine old Marc de Bourgogne is a kind of spirit compost, smoulderingly earthy;

a fine old Marc de Champagne is lighter and sappier, yet the vigor of its raw materials provides a typically driving finish.

There is one country whose marc is even more celebrated than those of France, as we will discover on the next two pages; look out, too, in Portugal for the local marc called bagaceira, and in Spain for the marc generally called aguardiente. If you see liquors labelled "Fine" in France, by contrast (such as Fine Bourgogne), this is not a marc but a brandy, distilled from wine rather than pomace.

# grappa

Grappa is Italian marc. The local word for pomace, the raw material of marc, is *vinaccia*. No wine-producing nation takes this piece of distillatory home economy more seriously than Italy: grappa is Italy's malt whisky, Italy's cognac, Italy's bourbon. The variety of grappe is almost limitless, and their distillation, too, is rarely carried out with as much craft as here. But there's more. Italians, famously, despise ugliness. In order to stress a variety palpable always to nose and tongue but seldom to the purchasing eye, Italian grappa makers send their spirits to market in a flotilla of exquisite, flask-like bottles. The result is that even a small collection quickly resembles an apothecary.

## discovering grappa

Much grappa is distilled from the pomace of a single grape variety (*monovitigno* in Italian). This is one of its greatest pleasures, giving drinkers the chance to meet the spirit shadow of old friends like Chardonnay, Sauvignon Blanc, or Pinot Nero (Pinot Noir).

Particularly showy are grappe produced from aromatic grape varieties like Moscato or Gewurztraminer. White grape varieties, since their skins are less "worked" in the winemaking process than red wines, often make grappa of more pronounced perfume than red grapes do. White grape pomace, too, is separately fermented by the grappa-maker. (For white wine, pressing precedes fermentation. For red wine, it comes afterwards.) The scent of sweet flowers (Moscato) or pounded rose petals (Gewurztraminer) can be arresting. The warm bite of the liquor seems, at first, a shock; as it subsides in the throat, the scents rise again like bees from a hive.

Other grappe can provide a wild spirit echo of Italy's great red wines, like Barolo, Chianti, or Amarone. The sensorial link will, in these cases, be less direct; the flavors are bruising and rustic.

Clear grappe are either "unaged," or have been aged (for extra harmony and oiliness) in glass. Color in a grappa indicates that it has been mellowed in wooden casks. Expect less primal perfume, a little more vanillin—and a much smoother ride.

*the scent of sweet flowers ...*
*or pounded rose petals*

# eaux de vie

The phrase *eau de vie* means "water of life." It is used in France to describe a distillate of any sort, but in particular the clear, dry spirits which are produced from a wide range of orchard fruits—as well as from fruits and berries gathered in the wild. The German term schnapps may describe such spirits, too. Limpid, pure, and haunting, these water-white drinks are essences. The blender's skill, here, counts for nothing: all that matters is the distiller's fidelity to often exotic raw materials.

## discovering eaux de vie

Cherries and plums are the two most popular fruits for eau de vie distillation. Kirsch is the name of the former; the latter tends to be labeled mirabelle, quetsch, or prune, depending on the type of plum from which it is made. (Slivovitz is the famous plum eau de vie of Central Europe.) The fruits are crushed after picking, then fermented and distilled; sometimes, too, the pits are cracked in order to give the liquor a kernel character. Once distillation is complete, the new spirit is aged in glass for a restful few months; it mellows in its jar without acquiring the color and subtle oxidation which ageing in wooden casks would bring. Eaux de vie are quick on the tongue, warming yet very dry, too, and leave the mouth scent-scorched after you've swallowed.

Pear forms the basis of another popular eau de vie, usually labeled poire Williams after the variety distillers prefer. The scent and flavor tends to be subtler and more fugitive than either kirsch or plum eau de vie. Framboise (raspberry) and fraise (strawberry) are both easily recognizable; mûre (blackberry) and myrtille (bilberry), rather less so. Juniper (genièvre), gentian root (gentiane), wood strawberries (fraise des bois), rowan berries (sorbier), holly berries (houx), elderberries (sureau), rosehips (eglantine or gratte-cul), and the berries of the wild service tree (alisier): all these are used to make obscure and expensive eaux de vie. In place of the easy charm of the fruit eaux de vie, those based on berries and roots tend to be sterner and more austere. Faithful, in other words, to a different natural ideal to that of the lush orchard: that of the tough, tenacious little plant in the lonely heights.

*... pure and haunting, these water-white drinks are essences*

# bitters

Modern liqueurs have evolved from the health-restoring herbal elixirs of the Middle Ages. The class of drink known as bitters never abandoned that tradition. They are, as the name indicates, bitter in flavor, made by macerating roots, herbs, seeds, and peels in spirit. Sometimes that bitterness is matched by sweetness. Sometimes it isn't: just close your eyes and gulp. Why, though, drink spirit which tastes unpleasant? To aid appetite and digestion, argue enthusiasts. Others feel that the rich concentration of apothecary plants from which bitters are made can lessen the anguish of a hangover. And then there are the masochists …

## discovering bitters

There are two types of bitter: those which are intended to be taken before a meal, sharpening the appetite, and those designed for drinking afterwards. Their recipes are secret. The pre-meal versions include the vividly colored Campari, in which orange peel plays a role (along with 67 other ingredients), and the yellow Suze, a sweet gentian-root bitter. Angostura, also based on gentian among other ingredients, is a bitter of such concentration that it tends to be used drop by drop, often in drinks taken before a meal—like a classic pink gin, made by adding Plymouth gin to a glass rinsed with a few drops of Angostura.

The after-dinner drinker has two main choices. One is to go for a "sipping" bitter: one in which the bitterness is not quite emetic, and is balanced with enough sweetness to make the experience a pleasant as well as digestively tonic one. Examples of this type of bitter include the hauntingly herbal Sicilian Averna and the slightly less concentrated Milanese Ramazzotti. The German Jagermeister is also palatably and sippably bitter-sweet, as is Hungary's Unicum. Bitters of this sort are generally bottled at 30% to 35% a.b.v. (though Unicum is 40% a.b.v.).

At the far end of palatability come the bitterest bitters of all, like Fernet Branca and Underberg, bottled and 40% and 44% respectively. Again, the ingredients are herbs and roots (Fernet Branca contains gentian, chamomile, rhubarb, licorice, peppermint, lemon peel, and saffron among its 30 ingredients); the intense bitterness is due to the balance and concentration of ingredients and a much dryer style. Fernet Branca has a mintier, slightly easier-drinking alternative called Branca Menta.

# liqueurs

Liqueurs, like bitters, owe
their origins to the potions
and medicines which monks,
apothecaries, and doctors
prepared to relieve the medical
miseries of our ancestors.
Some classical liqueurs, based
on roots and herbs, are little
changed since those days. Many
modern liqueurs, by contrast,
are richly sweet alcoholic drinks
based on fruits, confectionary,
or dairy products designed for
sipping after the end of a meal
or for using to mix cocktails.
Their variety is enormous.
The two elements common to
all are alcohol and sugar.
Liqueurs are always sweet.

# classic liqueurs

Classic liqueurs have certain elements in common. They tend to be based on an original and ancient recipe, and to include a wide number of (secret) ingredients. In the case of the greatest of all classic liqueurs, Chartreuse, Carthusian monks still supervise the liqueur's manufacture. The profits from its sale help maintain the vast monastery of La Grande Chartreuse, which occupies a remote valley high in the French Alps. In winter, snow falls; in summer, the mountain pastures are bright with wild flowers, some of which are collected and used in the liqueur. Through the watches of the night, by candlelight, those same monks pray daily for the spiritual health of the world.

Chartreuse contains 130 different roots, plants, peels, seeds, and flowers, and is available in different (naturally colored) forms. Green Chartreuse, at 55%, is a liqueur of explosive intensity and lingering complexity; Yellow Chartreuse, at 40%, is more honeyed and accessible. Both are available in V.E.P. form (the initials stand for Vieillissement Exceptionnellement Prolongé): these have been aged for around 12 years in large oak casks. The original Elixir is also available, packed in small ⅓ oz. (100 ml) jars inside a wooden canister; at 71% and with a much lower sugar content, it is not for drinking neat but can be dripped onto a sugar cube or diluted in water.

Other classics of the liqueur world include the herbal Bénédictine (whose ingredients include ferns, vanilla, tea, and myrrh), the orange-based Cointreau and Grand Marnier (the latter is blended with cognac), and the Scotch-based Drambuie and bourbon-based Southern Comfort. The Italian Strega (which is colored with saffron) and Galliano both use a variety of herb and plant ingredients —and lots of sweet syrup.

## new classic liqueurs

Imagination provides the only limits to the liqueur-maker's art. Sugar and alcohol both preserve. With them, the essence of any fruit, any nut, any seed, even any flower can be lifted from its original, natural home and gently laid to rest in a sweet, sipping solution.

Of course there are changes: modern times and technologies have, in particular, brought the richness of cream into the equation. In Britain, the biggest selling liqueur is no longer a monkish classic, but Baileys Irish Cream, invented as recently as 1974. This mixture of cream with Irish whiskey and subtle chocolate and coffee flavors has been much imitated, but never equaled. The possibilities opened up by the use of cream in liqueurs, though, has given rise to another new classic: Amarula Wild Fruit Cream, a South African alternative based on the softly peachy fruits of the amarula tree. It is every bit as good as Baileys.

Modern liqueurs have, in times of high excise duties, tended to emerge onto the market at a lower alcoholic strength than the classics. Midori, for example, a green melon liqueur produced in Japan, is bottled at 20%; and Malibu, a mixture of coconut and white rum, is 21%. Mozart is the discordant name of a chocolate liqueur made in Austria; the original version is just 17%. Archers Peach Schnapps is a little stronger, at 23%. The low alcoholic strength is a major reason why these modern liqueur styles are often unsatisfactory to drink on their own. They tend, consequently, to be used as ingredients in mixed long drinks and cocktails.

*imagination provides the only limits
to the liqueur-maker's art*

# after-dinner cocktails

Just as liqueurs give manufacturers a chance to express their creativity, so cocktails enable drinkers to put their imagination to work in creating new scents and flavors. The fact that most cocktails are drunk before a meal is no reason not to get the shaker to work after dinner, too. Fruity frivolity, of course, may no longer seem appropriate as night draws on. This is the time to begin assembling classic ingredients into sturdy, sipping drinks at the dryer and darker end of the cocktail spectrum.

## old fashioned

*A subtle southern classic.*

**2 oz. (50 ml) bourbon**
**½ oz. (12.5 ml) simple syrup**
**2 shakes Angostura bitters**
**orange peel, to garnish**

Stir the syrup and the bitters together with two ice cubes in a tumbler. Add half the bourbon and two more ice cubes and stir again. Finally add the remaining bourbon and a fifth and sixth ice cube and stir yet again; garnish with a twist of orange peel.

## godfather

*A cocktail you can't refuse.*

**2 oz. (50 ml) Scotch whisky**
**1 oz. (25 ml) almond liqueur or amaretto**

Shake the ingredients together with ice and strain into an ice-filled tumbler. A Godchild is made in the same way, using cognac instead of Scotch.

## brandy alexander

*Smooth and stylish.*

**2 oz. (50 ml) cognac**
**1 oz. (25 ml) chocolate liqueur (crème de cacao)**
**2 oz. (50 ml) light cream**
**grated nutmeg, to garnish**

Shake the ingredients together with ice and strain into a martini glass. Garnish with grated nutmeg.

## rum alexandra

*Coffee has never tasted this good.*

**2 oz. (50 ml) dark rum**
**1 oz. (25 ml) coffee liqueur**
**1 oz. (25 ml) light cream**
**coffee beans, to garnish**

Shake the ingredients together with ice and strain into a martini glass. Garnish with a few coffee beans.

## rusty nail

*A taste of the hills.*

**2 oz. (50 ml) Scotch whisky**
**1 oz. (25 ml) Drambuie**
**lemon zest, to garnish**

Stir the ingredients together with ice and strain into an ice-filled tumbler. Garnish with lemon zest.

## sidecar

*Open up the throttle.*

**2 oz. (50 ml) cognac**
**½ oz. (12.5 ml) Cointreau**
**½ oz. (12.5 ml) lemon juice**
**½ oz. (12.5 ml) chilled water**
**twist of lemon, to garnish**

Shake all the ingredients together with ice and strain into a martini glass. Garnish with a twist of lemon peel.

# index

**63**

## acknowledgments

The author would like to thank Sally Bishop, Sabine Cleizergues, and Catherine Manac'h.

The author and publisher would like to thank all the helpers at Berry Brothers & Rudd, Patricia Parnell and Byrony Wright. Thanks also to Robert Shackleton at 4 Princelet Street and Len at the Roost for their help with the photography.